AF479389

Do You Hear The Call

by

Sarah Dashew

©2019 Sarah Dashew

All rights reserved. No part of this book may be

reproduced or used in any manner without written consent by the copyright owner

except for the use of quotations in a book review.

First Edition, November 2019

ISBN 978-1-7342937-0-8

Cover photography by Nando Esparza

Cover design by Andre Botha

Published by Whistlefoot, LLC

www.SarahDashew.com

For my friend Janee,
who told me
I had a book in me.
And for Denise
because,
forever.

FOREWORD

Let's get something clear right off the bat--I do not think I am a talented visual artist!
When I was in 7th grade I took a painting class and painted a landscape with
trees of which I was VERY proud. I gave the painting to my mom, who, as all good moms
are, was supportive and appreciative. She displayed it in the kitchen. My friend came over
after school one day, saw the painting and said, "Oh how cute! Did you make that in
pre-school?"

I've always loved to doodle and draw, but I am under no illusions as to the objective
qualities of said doodling. I mean, my own wife can't even read my handwriting. But that
doesn't stop me. It feels good. I like it. It's creative. That's enough.

My dear friend Janee has been telling me for years I needed to write a book,
a children's book, something with drawings. I should make the drawings. Um, what?
But earlier this year a song came pouring out, a song that spoke to getting back to
the easy innocence of the child's enthusiasm about the world's creations and creating
the world. And the lyrics felt to me like a picture book.

So here we go. Here's the book. I love it, partially because the drawings are terrible.
They still came from me, and maybe that's enough.

But just in case you can't read my handwriting either, I've printed the lyrics to the song
on the next page. Sometimes it's handy to have a reference!

Here's to all the doodlers and off-key singers in the world; we need you more than
ever.

xox Sarah

DO YOU HEAR THE CALL

Come on in and sit with me
Whisper your stories or yell
Whatever it is that you can't keep in
What treasures you have to tell
Raise your hand if you understand
And then raise your hand if you don't
Get up and dance if you can't sit still
Or sit still, it's okay if you won't

Do you hear the call

I remember being little, digging in the dirt
I remember knowing I was small
But I remember knowing too that the world was big
And that we were a part of it all
Eating ice cream on a hot summer day
And then diving down deep in the water
How cold it got as you swam down deep
Coming up how it felt getting hotter

Do you hear the call

When will you answer

Come on in and sit with me
Whisper your stories or yell
The grasshopper that jumps from the grass to your knee
The butterfly that flutters so well

Do you hear the call

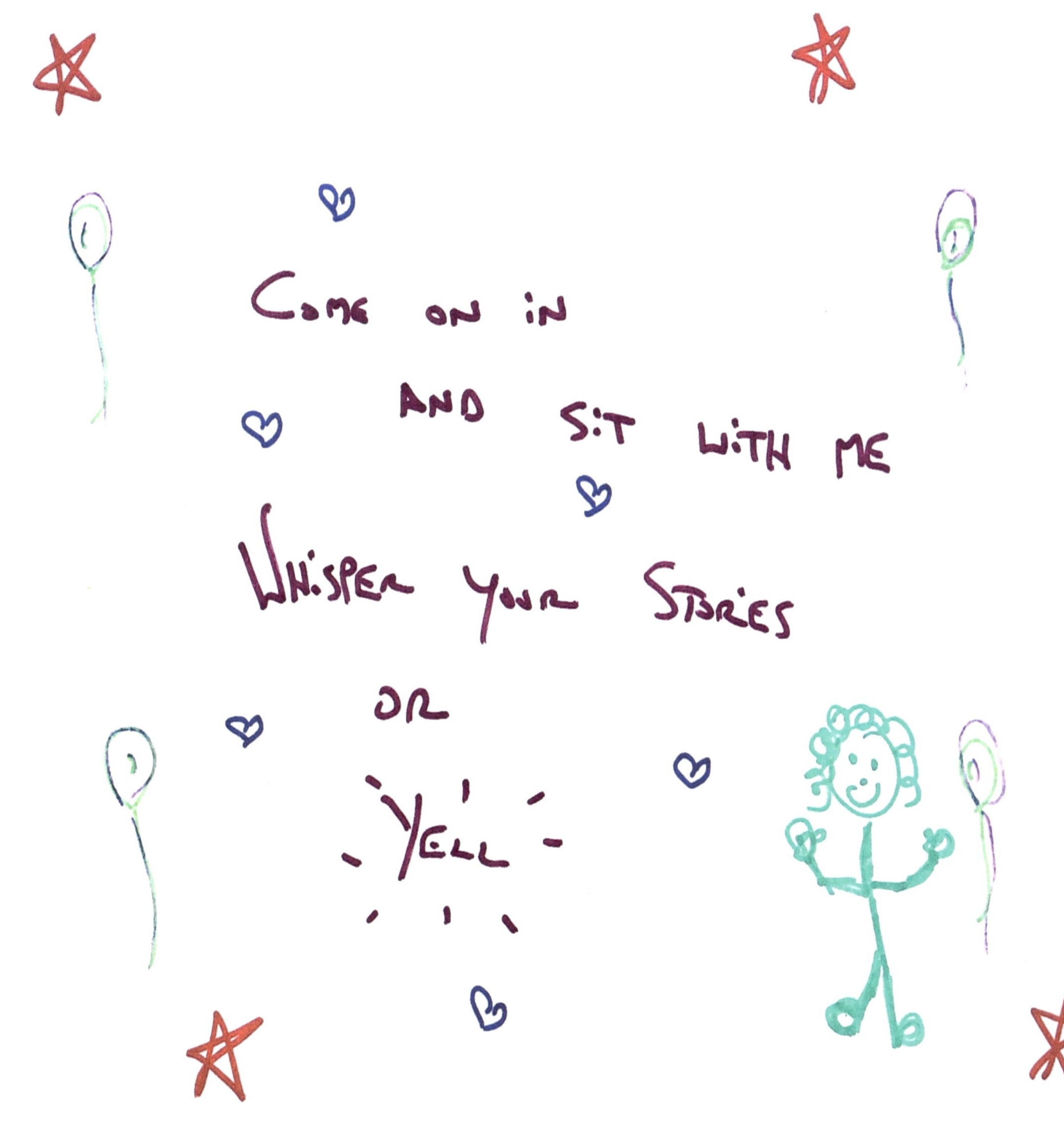

Come on in
AND Sit with me
Whisper your Stories
or
Yell

Whatever it is that you can't keep in

What Treasures

You Have To

Tell

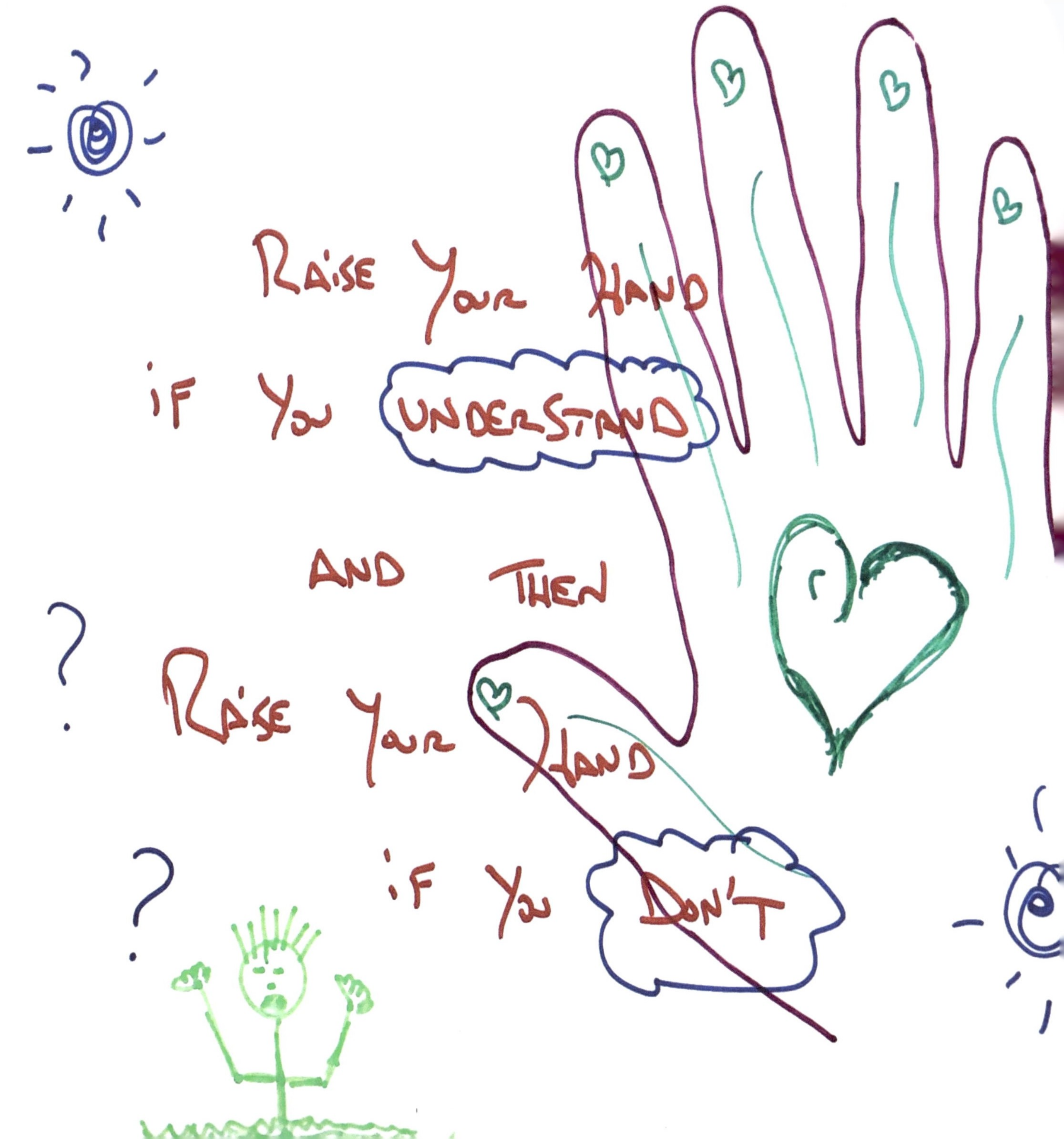

RAISE YOUR HAND
if YOU UNDERSTAND
AND THEN
RAISE YOUR HAND
if YOU DON'T
B
B
B
B
B

Get up and dance
if you can't
Sit Still

or
Sit Still

it's okay if you won't

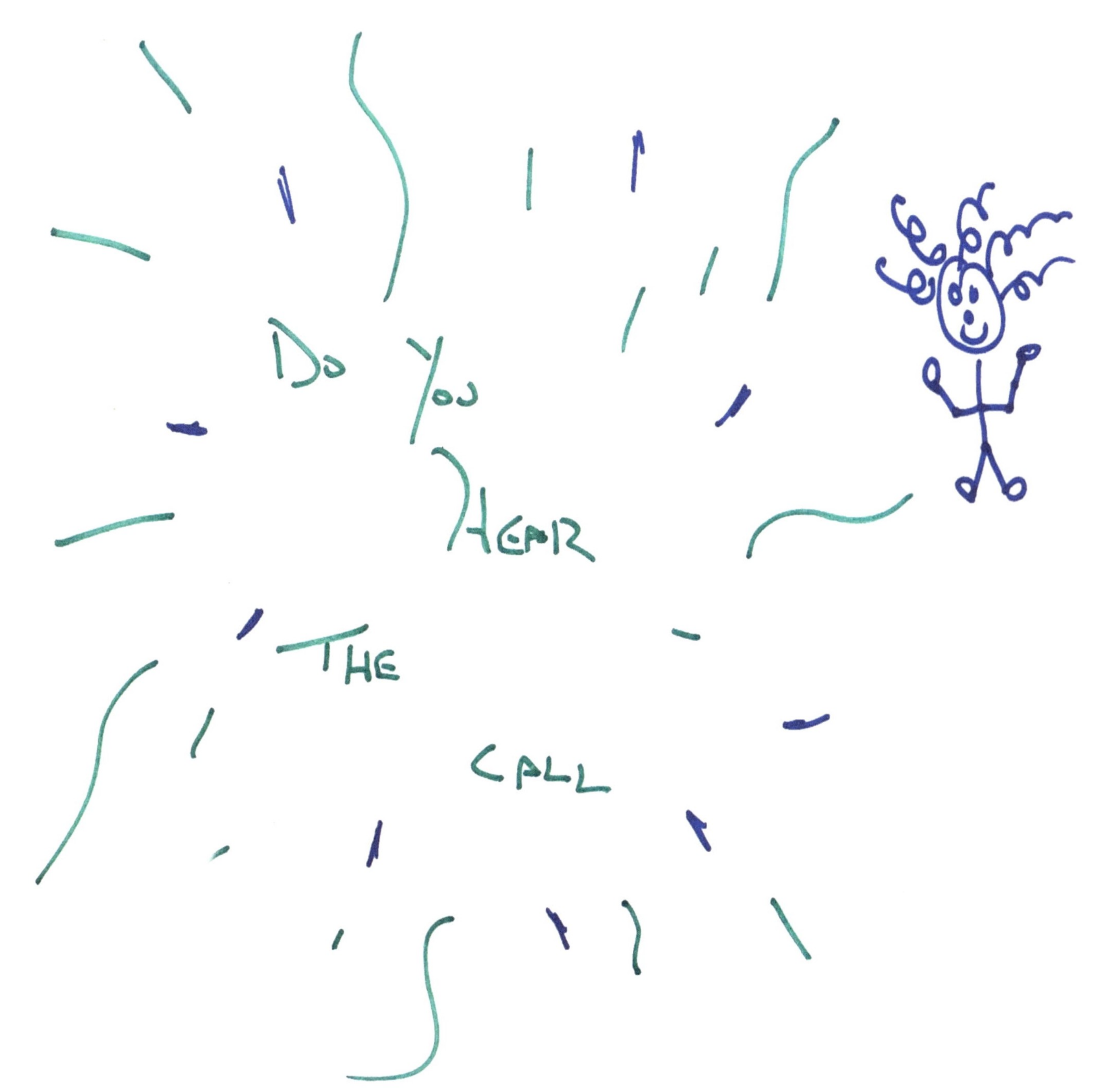

Do You
Hear
The
Call

I REMEMBER
    BEING LITTLE

DIGGING IN THE DIRT

I REMEMBER KNOWING
WE WERE SMALL

But I remember knowing too
that the world was big
and that we were a
part of it all

Eating ice cream
on a hot summer day
and then diving down deep
in the water

How COLD it got
as you swam down

Deep
$\overline{\overline{3}}$

Coming up how it felt

Getting Hotter
$\overline{\overline{\overline{}}}$

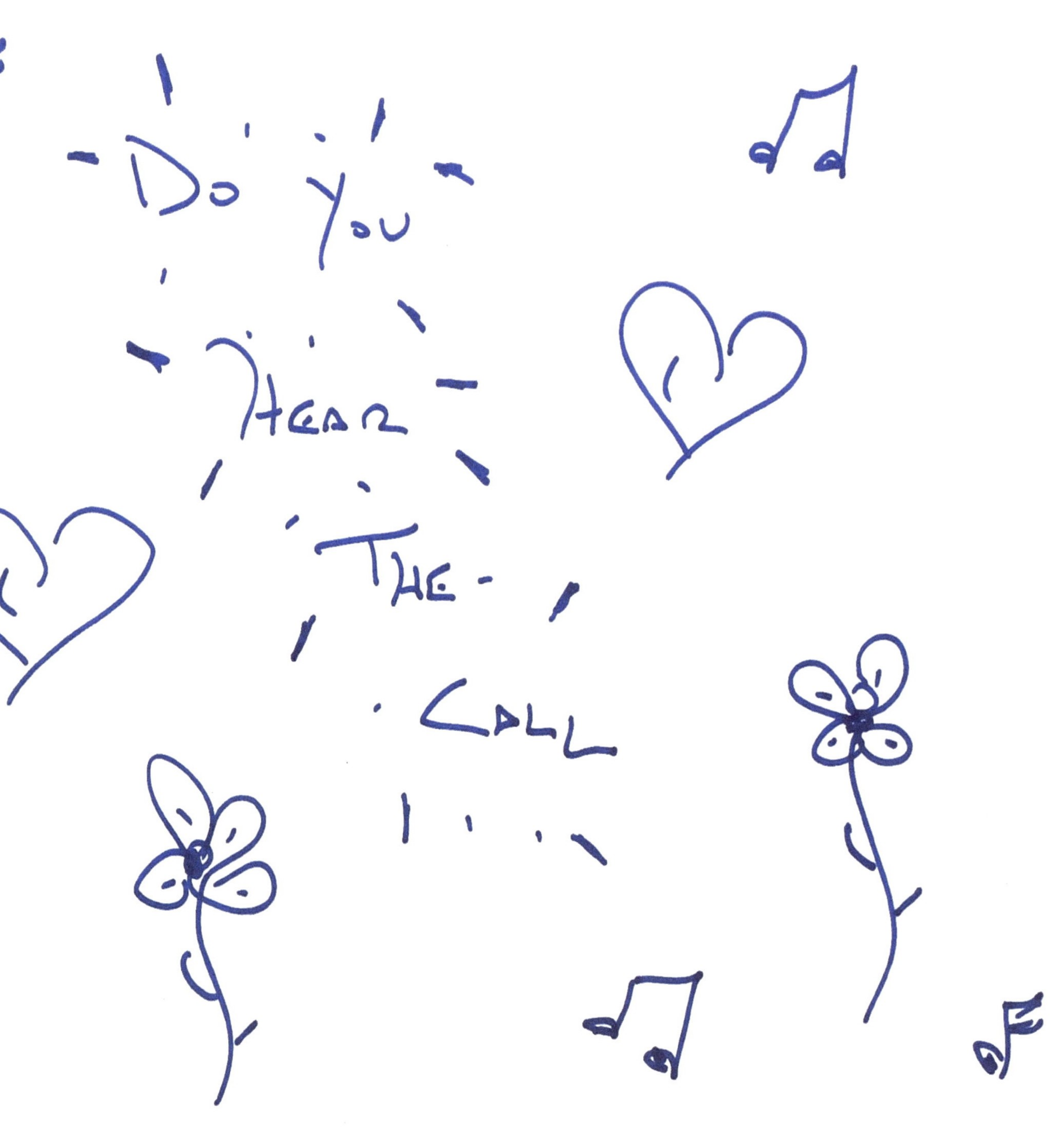

Do you
Hear
The
Call

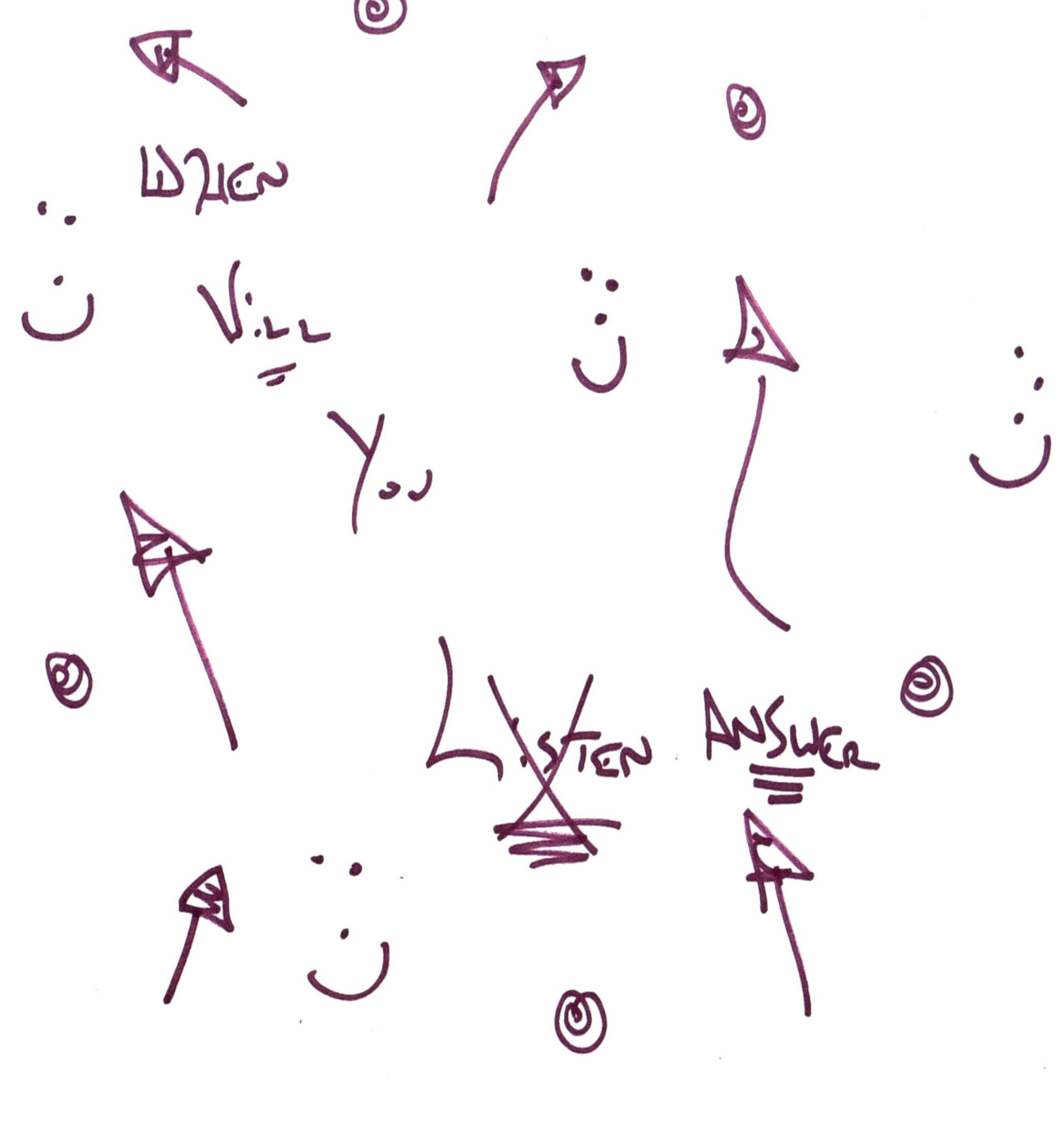

WHEN
Vill
You
LISTEN
ANSWER

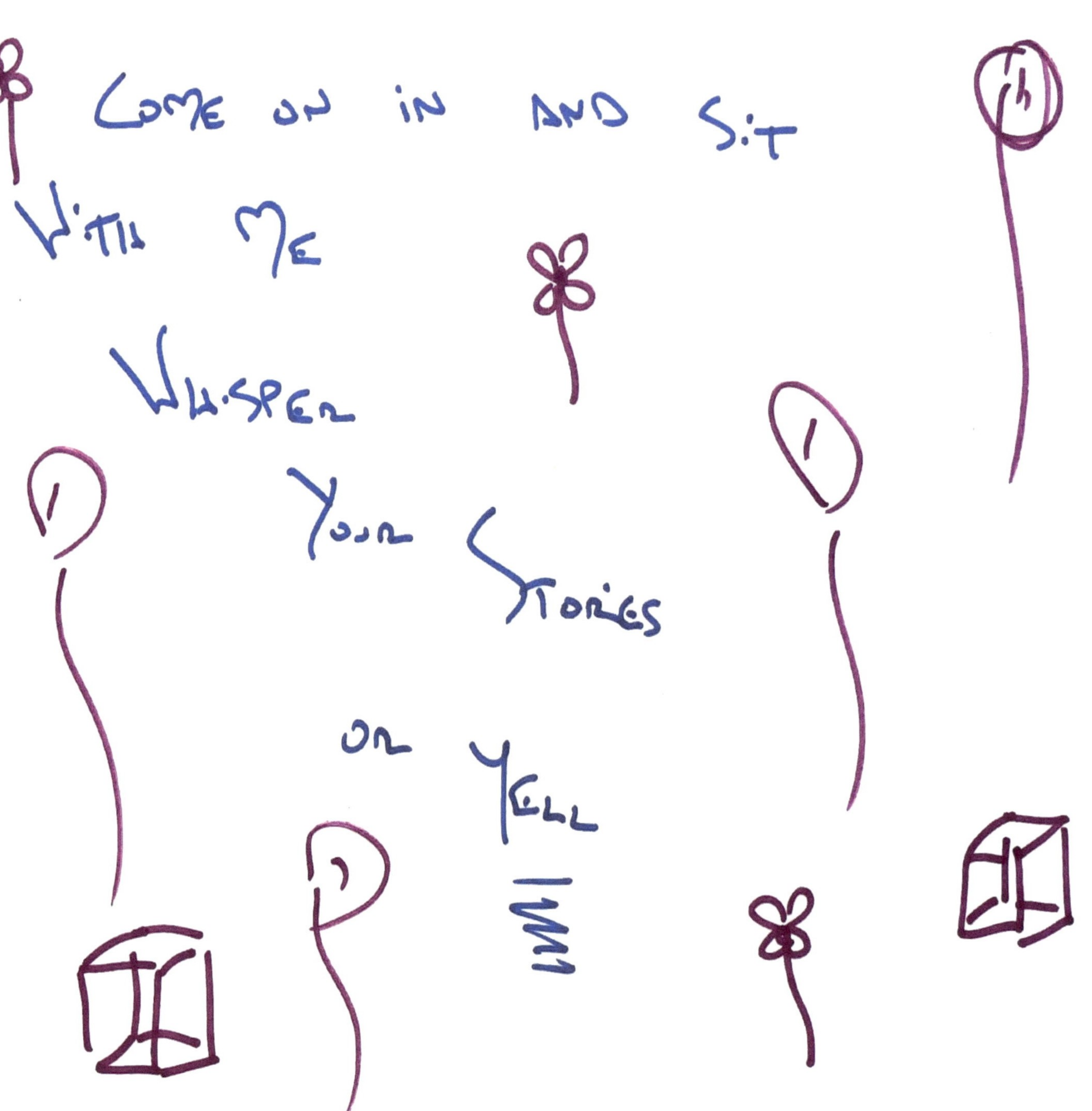
Come on in and sit
with me
Whisper
Your Stories
or Yell

The grasshopper that jumps

From the grass to your knee

The butterfly that

Flutters so well

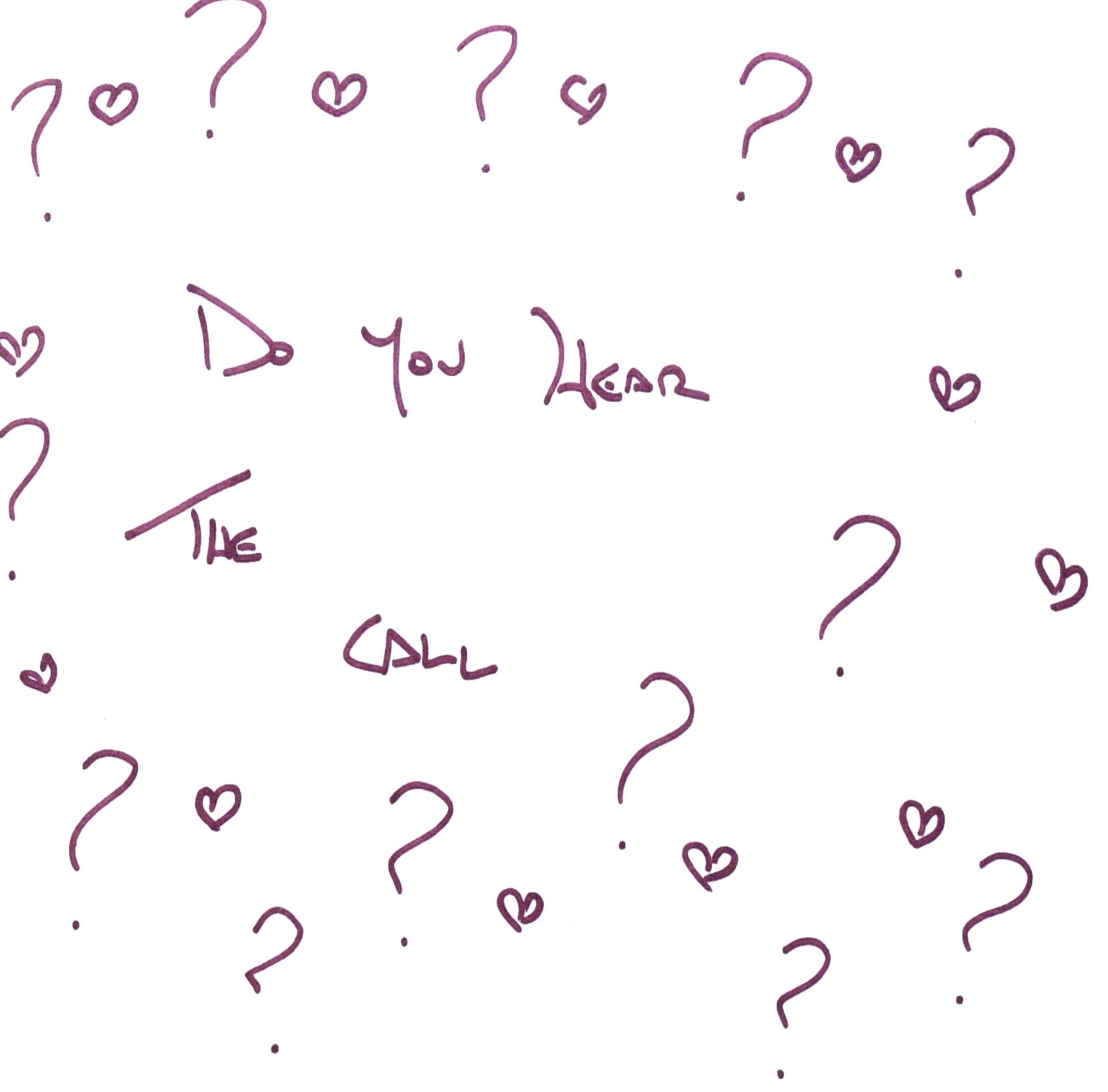

Do you Hear
The Call

It doesn't matter
if you can draw, or sing, or dance,
or waterski.
It matters that you try
if it seems like fun.
The experience is the thing.

xox Sarah

Go ahead and write or draw something!

Go ahead and write or draw something!

Go ahead and write or draw something!

Go ahead and write or draw something!

www.ingramcontent.com/pod-product-compliance
Lightning Source LLC
Chambersburg PA
CBHW041705030726
47636CB00013B/512